The Siege of Shoreham
Reflections From The Front Line

• Written by the protesters at Shoreham and their supporters •
• Edited by • Fiona Stephens • Wenda Shehata •

Cover design by Wenda Shehata & Fiona Stephens
Cover photographs by Roger Ockenden & Stewart Weir

Printed in the U.K. by
Impression Print & Design
24 Carden Avenue, Brighton.
England

Published by
HATAGRA Ltd (Publishing)
Brighton, Sussex BN1 4EJ
England.

This book is dedicated to all the people who care enough
to protest against the export of live animals from the U.K.

'O brave new world that has such people in it....'

Acknowledgements

The publication of this book has been made possible not only by the people whose work is included in the following pages, but by others who have contributed in so many different ways. They include:

Fiona Stephens
for her tireless efforts in getting information about this book
out to people and encouraging them to contribute articles.

Sean Currey
for the use of his photographs and time.

Roger Ockenden
for the "Siege of Shoreham" cover photograph
and those used throughout the book.

The Peace Centre, Brighton
for the use of their facilities.

M. Tucker, Harrow
for his encouragement and financial assistance.

Stewart Weir
for the use of his photographs, throughout this book.

Eden Akhavi
for his patience whilst guiding us
through the technicalities of production.

FOREWORD

"The world's history is the world's judgement", said Friedrich Von Schiller in his first lecture as Professor of History. The Siege of Shoreham is about both history and judgement because Shoreham will mark a turning point in our lives and future generations will judge the protests at Shoreham and elsewhere as events which brought about a new awakening in our care for animals. It will mark a time in history in which we became more human because we took animals more seriously. It will mark a time in history when we began to look at our responsibilities in a new light - for justice is brought about by struggle, education, shame, remorse and a change of heart and lifestyle.

Most struggles for justice - to end slavery or apartheid or to give women the vote, have involved a band of supporters who were outraged at the injustice being done and who made others hear what they didn't want to hear. That is the process of struggle and education. As the movements gained momentum they gained supporters and converts by shaming the people who colluded with the evil until individuals and society had a change of heart. Once a movement for justice gets under way nothing will stop it.

The protesters at Shoreham have my greatest admiration and support because they are opening the eyes of our country and beyond to the immorality of exporting calves to be subjected to the cruelty of crating. Beyond the issues of veal calves and sheep exports is the wider issue of our attitude to animals and the unwelcome truth that if we want to end the cruelty of factory farming we must either give up eating meat or be prepared to pay more for it.

The movement to ban live exports has much in common with other struggles to end cruelty. Ordinary people take to the streets, clashes take place with the police, people march and sing, they write poems and prayers, there are tears and laughter, hopes and disappointments, there is friendship and division, tempers and passions flare and arrests take place, the press give both support and criticism, people are injured or even killed but still the message spreads, and slowly but surely the issues are heard. Voices are raised in Parliament and the weakness of the opponent's arguments give way to the voice of humanity and justice.. In the end the law is changed, but still the movement moves forward for laws are not sufficient to change people's hearts and to make them hear what they don't want to hear and see what they don't want to see.

This is some of the history of Shoreham and in years to come when history is judged, we shall be able to hold our heads high and say, " I was there with them".

Dominic Walker OGS
Vicar of Brighton

INTRODUCTION

It has fallen to me as one of the people responsible for the publication of this book and more importantly, as a fellow protester, to write a few words of introduction to The Siege of Shoreham, though I am certain that it will speak for itself.

As the submissions for the book began pouring in, we waited hopefully for signs that our invitation to members of the Police Force, the 'Security guards' at the Port and the lorry drivers to contribute their stories, had been accepted...as far as we are aware, nothing has been forthcoming. So, for this reason, The Siege of Shoreham IS, as it was promoted, written by those who oppose the export of live animals.

Having read through this collection prior to printing, I can't help but wonder how, with the determination, love and hope that is represented here, we ever earned ourselves the title of 'thugs' and 'anarchists'? I am proud of 'us,' for in the face of adversity we have remained strong and have paid for our moments of weakness with dignity. Surely, the people responsible for this on-going atrocity must realise that they cannot win. Their recent, shallow victory in the High Court will be short-lived.

Personally, my one hope is, that never again will people believe that animals rights' is something that does not concern them. Every man, woman and child is responsible for ensuring a future in which our fellow creatures may live along side us, free from exploitation by Man whether it be for food, clothing, sport, entertainment or through experimentation. Animal abuse in any way, shape or form must one day come to an end, and in Shoreham, the sun has risen on that day.

Wenda Shehata

INDEX

ILLUSTRATIONS

WHO IS GUILTY?

Of caring about my fellow creatures
and for giving them a voice
Then I plead guilty.

Of attempting to obstruct the trucks of death
and for wanting to save their pitiful cargoes
Then I plead guilty.

Of venting my anger then causing disruption
and for questioning the law and democracy itself
Then I plead guilty.

Of accusing my fellow man of apathy and lack of conscience
and for shedding a tear and showing emotion
Then I plead guilty.

Steve Mallett

The Dunkirk Spirit Is Alive And Well, Living In Shoreham

I have spent the past week at Shoreham port where I joined the protests at the exporting of week old calves bound for the veal crates on the continent.

I went there with some trepidation, not knowing what to expect, this being the first time I have ever been to a demonstration; instead of finding fanatics and thugs, I found people very like myself, who have felt so sickened by what is going on that they are prepared to stand up and be counted.

The sight of the calves as they are rushed past is something I will never forget; they have a way of locking eyes with you, making you feel that you have bonded with one in particular, leaving you devastated by the knowledge of the hell that is waiting for it over the Channel. The sound of their crying stays with you for a long time afterwards with the knowledge that these creatures have just been taken from their mothers and all that they have known of life has been one week of happiness.

I can assure you that there are more pleasant ways to spend ones time than this. Standing in the cold for hours on end isn't the most palatable of pastimes, but the amazing thing is the spirit of the people down there is compensation for all the discomfort. Being there is restoring my faith in the human race. Every day I meet people with stories that warm my heart and give me hope that in these days of greed and selfishness the human heart is not impervious to injustice and suffering and is capable of extraordinary kindness.

An old lady of eighty nine years who hitch hiked miles to get there to lend her presence to the others; an old man in his eighties who comes every day, prepared to lie down in front of the lorries and risk his life for the animals. "Mine's nearly over" he said " But those little things haven't even started"; a young man with a bugle playing the last post across the harbour while the animals are being loaded into the boat; an elderly couple who come in their camper van every night and make tea for the demonstrators and a woman who lives opposite who is up all night offering tea and sympathy, as well as the use of her loo.

This is the thing that the British, once spurred into action, are best at; it's the Dunkirk spirit down there, alive and kicking and we mustn't let it die because if we can't do something to change this vile trade, then we are doomed to greed and indifference.

However, being an optimist, I believe that this is what we have been waiting for - the opportunity for the British as a race to join together and raise their voices in a cause that goes beyond race, religion or politics. Let us hope that these innocent creatures whose lives seem so worthless to those people who see them only as a way of getting rich, will be the means, through their indescribable suffering, of showing us that as a Nation we still believe in decency and compassion.

Joan Le Mesurier

Back For Tea-Time

There was a time when I found I could see
Through childs eyes the colours all around.
Tree and leaf and blue sky high above me
Feeling the softness of grass and ground.
And I could smell the sweetest air
See strange tin birds soaring in the blue
All touch and taste was wonderful to me
Within this brave new life I was born to.

I met with bees and butterflies and folk
Who gave me wisdom, taught me of life's ways.
In warm and yellow hay I ran and rested
For many many days.
And so I grew and learned security
Dependant on the way of human hands.
My mother gone and brothers, sisters too
I watched the humans sew and reap the land.

Once I was ill and felt the fear of pain
For many hours I lay in deep distress.
But the people made me well and from their care
A bond was formed within my happiness.
Oh joy when all that pain was gone
To gambol free and roll in soft green grass.
Life was so good when I was just a babe
What did they mean, it would not last?

Today's the day we're going for a ride.
Here comes the truck and up the ramp we go.
But why does sadness fill the streets
Tell them it's all for fun, for they should know.
We walked the sweet green fields and spent our days
And we don't recognise the fate you set.
Tell them, one day we will repay your kindness
Promise them, we won't forget.

M.T.F.

Them & Me

To them you are just a product, a way of making money.
To me you are an individual with a right to life.
To them you are a never-ending supply of cash with no feelings.

To me you are a fellow sentient creature with a family.
To the States Thugs in blue, who push, shove, punch, sneer and abuse,
 I am a violent anarchist.

To me who will not eat your flesh, wear your skin or steal your milk,
I do not care about their derision.
On Judgement Day, will you be with Them or Me?

Mark

I Stand...

I stand - soaked to the bone.

Banner of protest in hand.
Lorries loaded high with
Gentle - innocent creatures -
Made by God - not Man
                    Approach.

Eyes filled with fear and misery
Look down at me - appealing to me
To put an end - to their sickening plight.

I turn away - heart filled with sadness and
Outrage -
            At Man's indifference - and
My own - inability - to be able
To put a stop - to this
                    Heartless trade.

Meryl Tookaram.

Light By Battery

The Farmyard's looking empty
Everything's inside.
Sheep and cows and chickens
Have been taken for a ride.

Green fields aren't needed
A plastic shed is best
With a thing called a force feeder
To replace a Mother's breast.

We've always slaughtered Nature's Young
But now they're dying younger.
And we're not breeding milk fed veal
To stave off pangs of hunger.

For Noah's Ark they once queued up
To enter two by two,
We ship them by the thousands now
Cash bonus for the crew.

The lamb that's born in Springtime
Brought a tear drop to our eye
Now we're forcing plastic down its throat
It's it's Mother's turn to cry.

We can't tell fairy stories
Of furred and feathered friend,
We've forgotten what they look like
We are the living end.

So divorced are we from Nature
I'm sure she's had her fill
Of these two legged creatures
Who torture before we kill.

She'll never marry us again
We've murdered her you see,
And the Factory Farm's Special's
In the Top Ten on T.V.

Artificial Insemination
Now takes the place of a Dad.
And science tells us glibly
"They won't miss what they've not had"

Genetic Engineering
Will hold the key to Life,
Nature can be locked away
The Sperm Bank is your wife.

I gaze into the future
The fields are empty now,
And somewhere in the factory
They've bred a plastic cow.

It cannot moo, it cannot see,
It never had a Mum
It's a tasteless piece of rumpsteak
For us to feast upon.

Everything is covered,
There's no such word as sky,
Man's the only creature left
And he's afraid to die.

He finds a book left somewhere
And keeps on browsing through.
It's about a place called Eden
Where a thing called 'Light' shone through.

Andrew Ray

A Different Kind of Campaign

The shrill alarm clock jars me into wakefulness. A hasty coffee and a cold wash and it's off to the front line. A bit like the Army days with stand-to at first light, except that now the front line is at Hove Lagoon, and the enemy are not the North Koreans, but men in huge cattle trucks, carrying not troops but bewildered and disoriented hoofed creatures bound for incarceration and death.

Once again the long period of waiting for action, followed by the sudden burst of frenzied activity but without gunfire and mayhem. The difference now is that our only weapons are our banners and our voices.

The yellow jacketed Bobbies seem friendly enough but have the same air of anticipation. They appear to share our disgust at the evil business we are confronting, but are unable to speak out against it. Some chat to us, some stand aloof, then suddenly, all are alert. The chopper circles overhead and just as suddenly, two yellow clad lines stand facing the angry crowd lining the road to the harbour. Silently, more yellow jackets file down the steps from the Kingsway to join the lines below. Now we see a phalanx of black clad police in riot gear filling the road, and behind them the hated trucks with their pitiful cargoes, with more riot police trotting alongside, ready to hurl aside those who would dare get in the way. The air is filled with the screams of 'shame on you' to the police and the truckers they protect, carrying their innocent victims of Man's greed to torture and certain death. Stony faced officers with camera trained on the crowd. Tears flow from men, women and youngsters alike, tears of grief, rage and frustration. Then the last truck disappears out of sight heading for the wharf. The crowd falls strangely silent, perhaps in anti-climax. As the yellow coats file back up the steps there is an outbreak of jeers and catcalls, like a soccer team leaving the field after a game gone bad.

This is Britain in 1995. I wonder - What happened to all my cherished beliefs and youthful ideals. Is this really a glimpse of the future??

Bernard T.Denyer.

A Cry for Help

Little brown calf, when you looked out at me,
I took a photo of you in my memory.
I never will forget, your innocent sweet face,
You're caught in the system, of this barbaric disgrace.
Your life is only one week old
And mine is many years.
You're punished for doing nothing.
Can you see my tears?
Don't they see your misery?
Don't they see your need?
How can people buy God's creatures
And sell them for their greed?
Words cannot describe
Or in any way express,
My anger, my heartache,
My utter distress.
Please be brave my little one
Whatever they must do.
They may have no feelings,
But I will never forget you.

Adele Mathieu

Winds of Change

The winds of change are in the air.
It's time to stop this cruel nightmare.
Over one hundred years of trade have gone,
And still those cattle trucks roll on.
While occupants with mournful eyes,
They can but listen to the seagulls cries.
No green grass fields, no dawning day,
No chance to run and jump and play.
No mothers love, just freedom dreams,
We listen to their soulful screams.
The traders smirk and stand so proud,
They cannot face our caring crowd.
The time has come to show we care,
We must not witness more despair.

Katarina Williams

If Animals Could Understand........

Dear innocent animals, I wish you knew
Our dedication for saving you.
Don't hate us all - most of us care,
It's the powers that be, who are unfair.

When seen in those trucks - our hearts always break,
We shout to the word - WHY? For God's sake!
Your soul-searching eyes are greatly appealing
You make us all cry - your pain we are feeling.

There is no answer - there is no excuse
For the terrible way you suffer abuse.
Your lives are so short, since money and greed
Are the upper most thoughts of a certain breed.

One day in the future, cruelty must cease
And when Hove and Shoreham get back to peace
I'll look once more, to the Harbour again
And know that our protests were not done in vain.

It's then we will say, we knew we were right
In showing the world your terrible plight.
Time will enlighten, those foolish at heart
Who thought we'd give in and quietly depart.

Dear innocent animals, if only you knew,
We'll be there for ever, campaigning for you.
NOT now and then, but again and again,
Till you have a future, devoid of all pain.

Julie Ray

Friday Afternoon at Shoreham Harbour

I walk down to the sea, across the lagoon, past men in uniforms who stand and wait. As I look out to sea, the tidal waves roll in, and on each roll my eyes fill with tears. I walk back to stand with the others. I am with friends. There is a buzz, an air of anticipation, an air of dread. Then, as if some death knell has been sounded peoples faces turn. An eerie stillness and quiet descends upon us, fills the air and hangs around us. A whistle blows and on the horizon they come.

The uniforms, moving, walking slowly at first, then like a poisoned arrow, running alongside the cattle trucks. Helmets on, visors down, arms ready to push us aside like fallen bracken. Each truck slowly jolting forward. I can see the animals, they can see us. They plead for help, they cannot speak, but their eyes are a window to their souls. I cry, uncontrollable tears, sobs tearing through my body. I look at the men in uniforms. I had respect once. I turn and look into the lens of an Evidence Gatherer.

I am evidence.

Evidence that this atrocity exists on our shores.
Evidence that people do care!

Katrina Williams

I Pray

I sat and shed my heartfelt tears
As I watched the animals with their dreadful fears
I knew my tears weren't finding the answer
I prayed to God to be a dancer.

One who flew to where fear was rife
So I could explain their coming new life
Where love was all that would be felt
Not the beatings from leather belts
Where they could be with their mother
Not watch the death of their frightened brother.

I pray to God, help me give them hope
That beauty and green grass is on the next slope.
No more metal railings and being hung by rope
But dignity and respect and a loving stroke.

And as I sit looking in their eyes.
Give me the strength God, to help them survive.
Through all their hurt in this painful sham,
Not once do they ever judge man.

Love, acceptance and life
Is what God gave.
Hallelujah, let all be praised.
But most of all God,
Help the animals be saved.

Chris Matthews

A Protesters Prayer

'Running the Gauntlet' is a term adopted by a group of protesters, who until recently would run between the central reservation and the convoy, alongside the trucks for the length of the Kingsway, down Wharf Road until the convoy turned at the roundabout behind the Adur pub. Many would latch on to one driver, pleading with him to turn back or vent their anger and frustration on him for doing this work. It has become increasingly difficult in past weeks, due to a change in policing tactics and attitude, but every day that the cry "Convoy" goes up, they are there, to run as far as they are allowed. This prayer is dedicated to these brave men and women - may God keep them safe.

Dear God, give me the strength to run the gauntlet one more time,
Let me not tire at the green bubble
Nor fall prey to the men in black, before my task is complete.
Let there be hope in my heart and belief in what I do,
For it is right and just.
Don't let the animals be frightened by our shouts and the noise of our whistles
Shield them from the wails of the women and the anger of the men as they pass by,
Comfort them and help them understand that they have done no wrong.
And when I see their faces, looking out at me,
Father, don't let me cry.
Give me strength to dodge the police cameras and the lamp posts in my way,
Help me to know when to step up and step down,
And should I stumble on a kerb,
Oh Lord, don't let me fall.
Guide me as I run, so that my eyes may never leave the face of the driver with whom I plead to turn back.
Take the pain from my body as I feel the blows and pushes levied at me for getting "too close"
And God, when I know that all is lost and another convoy has got through,
forgive me, that I failed..

R.S.J.
Shoreham

People Power
© M.E. Austin 1995

Message to The People
© M.E. Austin 1995

A Trouble Shared

Oh Shoreham, your pain is transparent
The world is wet with your tears.
As the lorries of shame come into your port,
You weep and cover your ears.

These lorries of death, blood money on wheels,
Are a blight on all human kind,
Their cargo should be running free in our fields,
Not leaving this country behind.

You try not to listen as young babies cry,
And you cannot believe what you see.
There is nothing to offer those questioning eyes
That are saying "What's happening to me?"

Emotions of anger, frustration, are there
From people from all walks of life,
They come far and wide to show that they care,
There's a Doctor, a Lawyer, old man and his wife.

They stand so quiet as the lorries pass by,
Protected by those they thought friends.
Sometimes, they are hurt, but they'll be back again
Until this disgusting trade ends.

Oh Shoreham, we'll help you in your desperate plight,
We shall be there beside you each day.
More and more people will join your fight,
Until all your pain goes away.

A fight is for winning and that's what you'll do.
The day is not too far ahead
Your streets will be clean, you can start life anew,
No more to wake up to that dread.

Sally Scott

Through the Eyes of an Innocent

It's early morning and soon 'they' will be coming for us.
We are still so tired from our long journey,
Oh, so very tired, but nobody seems to care.
They've put us in a place called a lairage until we are on the move again.
The parting from our mothers is more than we can bear.

We are going to a place called Shoreham, we heard the truck drivers say.
We were pushed and shoved and prodded
Until we are packed in oh so tight.
It is hard to breathe and we are frightened,
Oh Mama! This cannot be right.

We are going down a road called the Kingsway,
And Mama, the silence is so loud.
We wonder what is happening and now we see the crowd.
They run up and try to stroke us, their eyes are full of tears,
We know they are trying to save us, and we know that somebody cares.

Oh Mama, they've been pushed away by men in black and yellow coats.
They must hurry, hurry, hurry, because
We have to sail when the tide is high.
The people who tried hard to save us are here,
Oh Mama, they have come to say 'goodbye'.

Mama, we know there is a Heaven for us,
We'll play again in grass so green, under skies forever blue.
These cruel, cruel men don't believe such things -
All they know and care about is money.
One day, Mama, they'll know that what we say is true.

Rosemary Pritchard-Williams.

Let The Convoy Through
© Sean Currey 1995

The Northern Cruiser
© Roger Ockenden 1995

Too Much To Bear
© Stewart Weir 1995

March Against Live Exports
© Roger Ockenden 1995

Speech by Cllr. Tehmtan Framroze, the Mayor of Brighton, at St. Peter's Church, Brighton on Saturday, 18th February 1995.

Good morning everyone. I'm delighted to see so many of you have made the journey here today to show your concern over the treatment of our fellow creatures.

I would like to start with a story; I was born in Zanzibar, off the coast of Africa. In the middle of the town in which I grew up there was once a market. But it wasn't the sound of cattle that filled the air from this market place, it was the sound of human beings....in chains... being sold and transported across the sea.
Yes, it was a slave market. On that site there now stands an Anglican church.

I recount this story because it seems to me that it is an appropriate moral tale for our times. For me one of the great moral issues of the last century was the slave trade; the appalling maltreatment and degradation of human beings, condemned because of the colour of their skin. This trade was finally abolished by an act of Parliament, and policed by British gunships off the coast of Africa - after much peaceful protest across the length and breadth of this country.

I believe that one of the great moral issues of our times is the appalling maltreatment and degradation of animals, most clearly expressed in the export of live veal calves from ports around our coast. Just as the people from Africa had once been exported from the coast of Zanzibar.

That is why I visited Shoreham to see for myself what was happening. I saw a convoy of animals being shipped to France to either be killed or reared in crates. I spoke to many people peacefully demonstrating against this trade. On my return I thought there must be many more people who would like to express their concern - but were perhaps unable to travel so far at night, or were perhaps put off by the television coverage showing isolated scenes of violence that distorted the true picture of largely peaceful protest.

Around the same time Brighton Council unanimously condemned this trade, with support from both political parties.

Daily, the Evening Argus was filled with letters from outraged local people, appalled at what was being done to innocent animals for private profit. It was also clear that our local police felt caught apparently defending a trade which, as individuals, many of them abhorred. They are only upholding the law, but inevitably many people have not seen it that way.

All of this led me to ask Canon Dominic Walker if we could take the unusual step of holding a special service in Brighton Parish Church. A service in which the town's religious and civic leaders could join together with local people of all faiths - and none - to reflect peacefully on our treatment of animals. I am delighted to say that Canon Dominic Walker readily agreed to my request. So we are here and, I believe, we are making history of a sort.

We are a part of the movement sweeping this country which clearly says that *enough is enough*, that not every decision in our society should be mad simply on the basis of private profit. That social justice for all our people, that care for our environment and it's safety for future generations, and that rightful concern for the other creatures with which we share this planet MUST form part of the decisions we make.

For without that I truly believe we are not fully human ourselves. Which is how we now view those slave traders in Zanzibar and elsewhere.

Will future generations look back on us now as we do on them and ask -
    "how could they do that?"

As Mayor of Brighton I pledge to do all that I can to persuade everyone that this trade is IMMORAL and therefore should be stopped NOW.

Thank you very much for listening to me.

I believe that together ...
peacefully ..
we WILL end this trade.

Reproduced with the kind permission of:

*Cllr. **Tehmtan Framroze**,*
Mayor of Brighton

Section 4

I have been protesting at Shoreham since 2nd January. Like many other people I had never protested about anything before although I knew I should have done. This time it was different. I have seen things during this protest, I thought I would never be witness to; people arrested for throwing orange peel, a sweet wrapper, for lobbing an egg at a driver who was laughing at us as he passed. Knowing what is possible down there, it came as no surprise that on Friday 24th March, I saw an elderly woman in her sixties pushed over by a policeman before the convoy came through. A fellow protester helped me pick her up and check that she wasn't too badly shaken.

When the lorries arrived at the traffic lights at Wharf Road, I, like most of the others was shouting at the drivers of the vehicles, who as always were well protected by the lines of police either side. Suddenly, a scuffle caught my eye - the same elderly lady who had fallen foul of the law before was being pushed over again. Instinctively, I ran to her assistance and remonstrated with the officer - maybe none too courteously - "Leave her alone, you bastard", whereupon I was arrested by two police officers ably assisted by five others within seconds. The 'lift' to the police van was none too pleasant - my head was hit several times on the Kingsway before I was thrown into the back of the van. My 'punishment' began there. Instead of being taken to a police station (with the others who had been arrested), we were driven to the lock, where we had to sit and watch the animals being loaded onto the Northern Cruiser! Talk about rubbing salt into the wounds - having to witness the one thing that we wanted to stop happening! I wanted to explain to the arresting officer that the woman who I had tried to help was about the same age as my mother and that I could not stand by and see any elderly person in that situation, without wanting to protect them. To try and make my point, I asked him if he would have treated his mother in the same way. He replied " It depends on what she was doing at the time".

My main concern was my wife, who did not know that I had been arrested and would be wondering where I was as she too was protesting against the live exports... Having heard that I had been arrested, she was driven to Brighton Police Station by another protester, where she'd been told I'd be taken, but at this time I was still at the Lock. Eventually, I did end up at a police station - Hove, not Brighton. Several hours later, my wife was able to collect the keys to our house which I had on me. She had been chasing around trying to find me and our nine month old son was by this time, hungry, cold, tired and wet. Very wet.

It wasn't so much being arrested for helping an old lady that upset me, but the fact that my family were also being punished. It is so sad to think that because we are protesting against something so terrible that we are thought of as anarchists with nothing better to do. We are judged by being down there. No thought is given to what we are as individuals.

I was duly charged under Section 4 of the C.J.A. and have since been refused Legal Aid, even though I receive Income Support. Furthermore, I have been told by a solicitor that the reason we are being arrested on such minor charges is to exclude us from the area on bail conditions. I suppose if it hadn't been me, it would have been someone else.

This just appears to make a mockery of our justice system!

M. C. Measor

Ship of Shame

The Northern Cruiser's through the lock,
huge crowds of us stand there in shock.
Satan's inside that captain and crew
Why did Shoreham ever let it through?

Across the basin and beside the canal side
trucks with their trailers and drivers who hide,
ten rattling and bouncing trucks speed along to the boat
crammed full of calves, but the drivers just gloat.

I think they are getting a great deal of money,
which helps pay their mortgage and make life more sunny!
While the calves and the sheep don't even get water
and end up in crates until they go to slaughter.

Now the trucks enter boat into the hold,
but the last one doesn't feel so bold -
There's not enough room, so he shunts back and forth,
in the meantime protesters are shouting in wrath!

Those poor animals are being thrown about,
It's no way to treat them, of that there's no doubt.
At last he's got in, now the ramp's closing up,
the drivers have gone, up on deck for a cup!

Is the hold black as hell? Is it cold? Below water?
Diesel fumes? Not much air? Not so good in that quarter?
The boat's going out now, it's turning around,
Our hearts are with the creatures, though our feet are on ground.

When the boat reaches France, the cattle unloaded,
Some cannot walk, and so they are goaded
Picked up, and thrown upon the ground,
Some injured, some dead, all treated rough it's been found.

We've got to stop this evil trade,
Make Shoreham once again 'top grade',
Meanwhile, don't leave the cattle in the lurch,
Pray with Dominic in St. Peter's Church!

Mary Belton

If a Calf Could Talk.....

No more to romp on pastures green
No more the daylight to be seen.
The end is nigh, I'm out of luck
Sent away in a rumbling truck.

I'm very young and know not why
I cross the sea to Hell and die.
What <u>did</u> I do (I'd like to say),
To offend such people in this way.

If I could speak, instead of moo
Perhaps the likes of you and you,
Would know that I am feeling pain
But as a calf, I can't complain.

No time to romp, on pastures green
No more the daylight, to be seen.
No time to graze or see the sky
A crate awaits, and I must die.

Julie Ray

We're Quite Safe - There's A Policeman
© Sean Currey 1995

Friday Afternoon - Hove Seafront
© Sean Currey 1995

Port Security.....?
© Stewart Weir 1995

**The Man We Loved
To Hate**
© Stewart Weir 1995

A Salute To The Brave Lads Of Shoreham Port Authority
(in the manner of the immortal bard, William McGonagall)

Now McGonagall was a man who knew something about writing verse,
And if I take on his mantle, I hope that from beyond the grave he will not
visit me with a curse.

I am here to sing the praises of Shoreham Authority Port,
Although some disgruntled people think they are really not doing what they
ought.

Because if they don't ship live animals abroad, they won't raise any cash,
And the Harbour might end up, like the power station chimney, with a big
crash.

They are entirely within the law - even if some of their operators aren't;
And, anyway, someone else will do it, if for any reason Shoreham can't.

They can't think why there's so much fuss at going for fifteen hours, at best,
Without food, water, or any kind of rest.

Why, along at Shoreham Port Office they often go for two hours without a
cup of tea,
And if they're really pushed, they can stretch it out to three.

So the Port Authority wants in the live export trade to make itself a name;
And I've got a kind of feeling they're going to be successful in that aim.

Fay Marshall

The Black Hand Gang

Because you wear a uniform
You can punch me in the chest,
And kick that old man down the street
Snarl and curse at all the rest.

Because you have a number
You keep hidden from our view.
You think that gives you licence
To do the awful things you do.

Because you're here in hundreds
And protect each others backs.
You believe that we are vulnerable
And open to attack.

Old ladies look at you with hate
And still you wonder why.
You've got officers who snigger
At the people when they cry.

You ask us why we're doing this
And tell us "You won't win."
But we'll face you and your dark army
No matter how many you draft in.

Just doing your job, you tell us
As you protect this evil trade
Although we're all in this together -
We're not getting paid!

Bruised & Confused
Brighton.

My First Shipment

Well, I'm here. I've finally plucked up enough courage to stand and protest. I am so confused. How am I going to feel? I just don't know yet.

Cries from sad hearts go up - " The animals are coming!" My stomach churns, my knees shake, I feel physically sick as the huge convoy comes into view. I glance around and realise from the wide-eyed looks of horror on other faces, that they too are feeling the same emotions as I.

The massive police presence escorting the convoy into town totally terrifies me. I have never experienced anything like this before. The animals reach me and I cry out at the shame of what we humans are doing to these sentient creatures. A liquid brown eye catches mine - a calf, no more than four weeks old stares back at me. I weep!! How can I explain that I cannot save him? Maybe in the future I can stop the pain and suffering of his descendants.

I walk away. The animals have gone through to the Northern Cruiser. From this day on, I know my life will never be the same again!

Juli
Worthing

His Last Words

Mama, where am I going,
I'm scared and fighting for my life.
Mama, I'm dying,
In pain and in a veal crate of frightened calves.
I'm dead and thrown overboard,
Washed up, for everyone to see ME.
Only those who care cry for me,
But others laugh and shake their heads
And don't lift a finger to help.
I was bleeding, dying and ......
IN PAIN.
Warm bodies beside me,
Dead, but not physically dead,
But dead in the MIND.
Lost in pain and wounded and laughed at by Humans.
Mama, I'm NEVER coming back,
And the others are NEVER coming back either.

Tamara Fernandez
Age 11

The Question is.......

It wasn't many weeks ago - a Wednesday or Thursday, if I remember rightly, just after the animals had been driven through and the memory of their confused little faces was still fresh in our minds .One of the police camera crew, apparatus in hand, made his way to a group of people standing down below on Wharf Road.

I don't know what was being said, but there were angry exchanges, lots of pointing from the policeman and animated faces in return from the protesters who gathered round. Whatever was happening finished fast and he climbed back up to the Kingsway to his partner. Before he got to the top, a young woman, wearing a green jacket and dark glasses walked forward and stood at the bottom of the slope. Her voice was clear. Not angry, but indignant as she shouted " You are OUR policemen. We are YOUR people. Why must you intimidate us this way?"

I suppose now, that she spoke for all of us there. She was asking the question that was on all of our lips. Why? Why are we being treated like criminals? Why are we being abused by people employed to look after us and protect us?

His answer? There wasn't one. He put the camera to his eye and began filming.

William Peters

Compassion
(People have everything, Animals have nothing, Please help them.)

Shoreham was a lovely place,
With river, hills and sea,
But wicked things have happened here,
In front of you and me.

We find it hard to sleep at night,
On what that day, we've seen
Those calves are only one week old
And have not had chance to wean.

The animals look so bewildered,
As the crowd gathers round the lorries,
But when they get to Europe
That would be the minor of their worries.

Some churches are very silent,
And preach of things gone by,
I only hope that God will help those souls,
From his pulpit in the sky.

The Tory farmers and hunting friends
Will have a great surprise,
When the rest of the people disown them,
For their greed, deceit and lies.

We are getting our act together,
With people from other ports
There's housewives, tradesmen and pensioners,
And many other sorts.

I've met some lovely people,
In the daytime and at night.
The sort that won't ever let you down
And will help keep up the fight.

So come on down to Shoreham,
And help our humane cause,
Because we will stand united
And sod the government laws!

But one thing to remember,
When we've stopped this evil trade,
We'll be the ones who can feel proud
Because we're the ones who stayed.

Jim 'Road Cone' Gumbrell

The Long Haul

At the beginning of January, when the export of live animals commenced at Shoreham (really, the Lagoon Entrance at Hove) I felt compelled to go to see for myself - what an eye opening experience! The worst part is to watch the lorries taking the animals through knowing their helplessness. Sheep packed in double layers, so tightly they cannot move. Some calves so small you can only see their ears, some a little larger straining towards the wooden slats on the sides of the lorries. The distress and fear obvious - their eyes say it all. The frustration and anger at not being able to help them. The best part is to meet, mingle and talk to likeminded people who care. They come from far and wide, men and women, young, middle aged and old not caring about the ice cold, very windy and atrociously wet weather either day or night, just to be there to say they care.

For the animals, the hunger, thirst, fear, distress and pain starts when they are taken from the farm (some are just factory farms). Some go to the markets. They are prodded and poked by indifferent men and sold to the highest bidder. Some animals, (the lucky ones) are bought by other farmers to be reared for further dairy use or fattened for beef, often in very poor conditions. The others start the journey to the veal crate, or in the case of sheep for slaughter in atrociously callous conditions as far away as Greece, Italy, Spain and Portugal.

As our Government and those in the background benefit from the rich pickings of this vile trade, and apathetically blame the European Laws and people, it is up to us, the general public, to object in every way possible to this unecessary cruelty.

Every little bit we do will help our fellow creatures out of the hell that they are going through.

Barbara Baker

GOD GAVE LIFE TO ALL THE ANIMALS.

A song composed by Gloria Macari and Roger Ferris for the concern of animal welfare. This song has been adopted by protesters against live exports at the Port of Shoreham.

People think they're so important
Living in their world of sin
Where does love come in?
Looking down on all the creatures,
They may be big or small,
But, He made them all.
We must learn before our life is through -
This is their world too.

CHORUS;

God gave life to all the animals,
Don't take it away, let them live another day.
He gave life to all the animals,
Don't take it away, let them live another day.
"We must learn before our life is through,
This is their world too."

2nd Chorus: "You will learn when your life is through,
                It was their world too."

Mothers crying, babies dying,
No-one ever see the tears,
They die in fear,
Where are rights if they can't fight back,
No-one ever takes the blame,
They die in pain.
You will learn when your life is through, it was their world too.

CHORUS:

3rd Chorus: God gave life to all the animals,
                Don't take it away, let them live another day,
                He made them all, creatures great and small.

R. Ferris/G. Macari © 1992

The "Veal" Truth

A baby sucks his mother's teat
Where from it milk comes warm and sweet
Maternal instincts bond them tight
The law of nature makes it right
The pain and suffering of giving birth
Has changed to joy and pride and mirth
She once was lonely - now she's not
Life's worth living with what she's got
The baby cries and mother calms
Compassion flows, they sense no harm
No-one should take this gift of life
That mother's womb has held so tight
"Bring back my baby!" is her appeal
But cow's young calf has gone for veal.

Dave Hammond

Sentient Beings

Sometimes people say "Why worry about animals? What about children and people?" I would say that compassion is not divisible. I do not know anyone who is concerned about animals who is not also concerned about children and people.

God gave life to *all* animals. They are sentient beings. They have characteristics, personalities, they feel heat and cold - and suffering.

We *all* have a responsibility to those animals.

Reproduced in part from a speech made at St. Peter's Church, Brighton
on Saturday, 18th February 1995 with the kind permission of:

Sir Andrew Bowden M.B.E., M.P.

The Siege of Shoreham

Forever Together

With me now,
with me forever,
through good times, through bad times
through stormy weather.
You are my friends,
you care like I do,
I'm proud to fight for animals
with people like you.

Never get sad,
never give in,
don't get down-hearted,
you know we will win.
I'm with you always,
deep in my heart
we'll keep up the struggle
'til death do us part.

An Absent Friend

Grannies From Hell

I wonder of any of you can help? I've been trying to find the frequently mentioned group 'Rent-a-Mob' in the Yellow Pages without success.

Some of us who have been at the Shoreham protests have the idea of forming a group called "Grannies from Hell" and hiring ourselves out for demos - in order to supplement our pensions.

Our only problem is we've not actually found anyone yet willing to pay us. Information please.

Fay Marshall
(First published in the West Sussex Gazette)

"For the Protesters"

In Another World, Another Place
I Will Look Down And Remember The
People Who Fought For Me,
Who Tried To Ease My Suffering,
Who Cried As I Was Shipped To My Prison,
Hundreds Of Compassionate Hearts
Beating To One Rhythm Of Release
And Freedom For All Animals,
Marching As One To Be Counted And
Stand Proud in Their Beliefs
Before All Who Allow This Trade.
The Compassionate Spirits Of All The
Protesters Will Unite Across
The Seas And Skies to End The Suffering.

PLEASE FIGHT ON FOR US!

BAN LIVE EXPORTS FOR ALL ANIMALS.

Jacqueline

A Day in the Life of a Protester

When attending the lobby of Parliament against the live export of animals, I was given a notice of a Protest March to be held at Shoreham on 4th March. Two friends and I decided to support this event and were exhilerated by the feeling of togetherness with other compassionate people.

After that day, together with my husband, we felt that we must support the protesters as often as possible. Living in Croydon, we cannot come daily, but do come at least twice a week.

Our first day, was a day to remember with utter sadness. Firstly, the noise and bustle around Hove Lagoon, then the ominous silence when the traffic was stopped. The blowing of whistles to herald the imminent arrival of the convoy. A sinking feeling in the stomach as in the distance you see the yellow coated policemen, leading in the transporters, filled with calves and sheep, doomed to a dreadful 'life' and death. As they pass, with tears streaming down our faces, we cannot believe man's inhumanity to the animal kingdom.

On our Shoreham days, life revolves around the high tide table, necessitating sometimes an early start to the day, but we will never give up, until this disgusting vile trade ceases. We will 'fight' in Parliament, we will 'fight' on the media and we will 'fight along the sea front, until we overcome!

Betty Swift

Hove Lagoon

It used to be a happy place down by the Lagoon in the sun,
Children playing, swings, ice cream, oh what happy fun.

How different now, cries of anger and abuse - animals in distress
In need of a drink of water and a proper rest.

Ordinary people of every age and way of life,
protesting at the evil trade of lorries,
Taking calves to short lives in a crate,
Sheep to death in a cruel and wicked fate.

What sort of men are these, who drive this evil convoy,
So well guarded by so many police?

This trade can be stopped so quickly if the will is there.
But most of our M.P.'s simply do not care.

To those who have protested, right from the early days,
I'm proud to stand beside them in these latter days.

God bless them all, in this great fight
Let's hope things are soon put right
That the town returns to peace and quiet.

The Lagoon, once more a place of fun
With families happy in the sun.

A Protester from Portslade

"Activist",
"Anarchist",
" Extremist",
"Fanatic" -

If that is what I am to be called,
because I care -

I shall wear each name with pride!

Annie
Age 82

Twelve Pieces of Silver

You're the nameless face I wait for every day, with your cargo of fear and its well trained guard.

I despise you and the fact you could be bought - Though no amount of money could justify what you do, you do it, nonetheless. Tell me, does every man have his price?

Arrogant in the safety of your glass case, sitting high above us, you peer out, laughing. While we, so far beneath your smug grin look up, to look down on you, in every way.

Shame on you and shame on what you do!

Carrier of death, harbinger of despair, you come into our port with your pitiful load and debase our town with your presence, day after day.

The passage of time will etch your wicked deeds deep into the hearts of every one who watches and you will never be forgiven. You, who have murdered morality with your greed, raped compassion and pillaged the dreams of a peaceful people, deserve no mercy.

You have sold your soul for twelve pieces of silver.

John P.
Hove

High Noon

Mr. Daisy, the wealthy cow
Bought a human lady
He wanted her for her milk
But knew she'd need a baby.
So he mated her for five years
Until she was exhausted
Then, after breaking her heart and soul
Sent her to be slaughtered.
But, during those long five years
She bore five baby boys
So he shipped them out to baby crates
'Couldn't understand the noise.
The other cows protested
And said that this was evil
"Can't understand the fuss" he said
"After all, it is quite legal."
"They're only babies after all,
and they belong to me
I'm making money, fair and square
It's just a factory."
"That's where you are wrong."
The other cows said
"We will stop you soon
Your trucks will roll by empty -
For you, it is High Noon!"

Sandy Tyler-Humm

Animal Cruelty

I think that the police should care. We only try to stop the lorries because we care for the animals. I care for all animals in the world. We need more people to stop the lorries and then we will have lots of baby sheep and cows in the world. I think the poor baby sheep and cows should be left free in the fields. On those horrid lorries baby sheep and cows want their mummies.

Roxanne Bryant
Age 6

Spy Cat

This is the story of Cat.......... no ordinary moggy but a top-of-the-range, very rare jet black Maine Coon....an Aristocat who shares his home with two other pussies - a breathtaking Silver Tabby Maine Coon and a very loveable floppy Ragdoll.

The Young black (Caprix Ebony) known as the Black Bomber has found a new and quite rewarding game....Shipwatching.

My lounge window faces the entrance to Shoreham Harbour and the Bomber and I spend many hours watching for the Red Hell Ship (the Northern Cruiser). As I live alone and have to sleep sometimes, the Bomber keeps lone watch and if *any* ship comes into the harbour entrance, he races into my bedroom and wakes me, getting cat treats as a reward. The only problem is that he cannot distinguish between different vessels so I often get woken for sand dredgers, but he is so good that he gets his reward anyway. - I really must attend to his training.

He is a wonderful ally and my three cats are my only reason for living apart from stopping this vile trade.

Good Luck to you all!

Sir Roger Sear

People Farm

When I go down to Shoreham
Reminds me of a book I read,
Written by George Orwell
About sheep being misled!

There was one wise old donkey
Plus a very willing horse,
Dogs were used to keep order,
The pigs in charge of course!

They ousted the wicked farmer
Together they would unite,
Working with pig-in-charge
A better future was in sight?

Pig made the new laws
Every animal would obey,
The donkey thought alot
But little did he say.

The sheep were then led blindly,
Rules were altered overnight,
Donkey knew what happened
They shut his mouth real tight!

Week after week, the willing horse
Had worked himself too hard,
Then one day exhausted
Was sent to the knackers yard!

The pigs had clearly lied,
The sheep had been misled
The animals were not equal
After all the pigs had said!

Based cleverly on politics,
This book filled me with alarm,
It's just coincidental,
The book's called "Animal Farm".

J.E.M.

A Calf's Lament

I cannot speak or say how I feel
There is just nothing I can do
What have I done to deserve this
I have never done anything to you

I did not spend much time with my mother
They just came and I had to go
I hear there are green fields to play in
But my life was too short to know

Yes, I did have a mother and I did have a life
But it was not for very long
For they came and took this away from me
And I wondered what I had done wrong.

I just wish they could see me crying
I wish they could see my tears
I wish they could feel how scared I was
I wish they could feel my fears

I do have a heart and I do feel pain
And like you I also cry
For I knew my life was over
And I was going to die

Just because I am an animal
I still have rights like you
So please stop this awful trade for us
Feel guilty for what you do

To the people who care and speak for us
You are our dearest friends
Do not give up, keep fighting hard
Until this cruel trade ends.

Nicola Rawlings

Nothing I Can Do!

There's nothing I can do
To make my dream come true.
Tightly packed in a cage,
Helpless and afraid.
I'm part of a legal trade,
(A cruel, evil trade.)
Being shipped from Shoreham Port
Over the ocean blue.

My dream is to be
In a field of green,
With my mother by my side.
But this can never come true...
For it's the turning of the tide,
And I can see no end to this nightmare ride.
The ship is about to depart.
Nothing can mend my broken heart.

Meredith Kenward
Age 12

Diary of a Virgin-Protester

2 am Tuesday, 2nd January.

I awoke to the radio news bulletin reporting that around 200 protesters lay in the road at the entrance to Shoreham Harbour and prevented lorry loads of live animals becoming a shipment to the continent. 'My God', I thought, 'I can't believe they've done it, that's amazing, I can't believe they've done it - What people power!'
The lorry loads of animals had to be turned back by police due to the united strength of the people.

Out of character for me, I leapt out of bed. I cycled down to the port to look for signs of the cause. I found two, 16 year old girls holding placards by the roadside who explained what had happened the night before and said, 'Please come down at 7 o'clock tonight, we are expecting the shipment at about 11 o'clock due to the time of the tide.'
I had to choose between going to a cosy college reunion meal, or braving the unknown, the cold and probably much confrontation with Police. But for the sake of the animals, did I really have a choice?

I attended the mass protest on January 2nd and joined the will of the community. I met hundreds of good people, courageous people and felt the euphoria at seeing seven lorries turn back after a stand-off of about an hour, when we held the lorries at a stand-still.

7 pm Wednesday, 3rd January

I am finishing my evening meal and getting dressed to attend my second night at Shoreham. I don every item of clothing I have that will fit over the previous layer - a bit like Russian Dolls.

I have journeyed home from work down the A23 and have seen signs of many police vans en route - I presume they are destined to face me at Shoreham. I am quite nervous of facing confrontation and the unknown. I am not psyching myself up- more psyching myself down. I am going to be a body, part of a crowd - not to be violent - but cumbersome.

When we reached the Harbour we knew it was a forgone conclusion that the convoy would succeed to the ship. However, what force we have warranted, thirteen hundred police, many in riot regalia and at a cost of £160,000 a day.

The ripples of our impact must be important... and spreading.

Watch this space.

M.J. Freedman

Policemans Lot

Hello, Hello, I am a policeman
It's a job I love you see,
Each day I put on my uniform
Orders, treat protesters inhumanely!

I go down to Shoreham Port
Showing my brutish might,
I witness animals in distress
Carted away and out of sight!

They know not where they're going,
Their journey long and hard
Reaching the end of the suffering,
In some foreign knackers yard.

It's not a nightmare, policeman,
It's really true to say: -
"The animals are really crated up
Treated in a most disgusting way."

Then the wonderful, friendly policeman
Can go back upon his beat,
Smile at all the old folk
And the children he'd mistreat!

Now you've received your blood money,
The Politicians have won the day,
Have compassion for your family,
Was the injustice worth the pay?

A.J.M.
Brighton

A Special Journey

We have one day, a special journey we shall make,
Along a well worn path, that path that everyone must take,
Friends, family, and those I've hurt, stand by the gate,
But - can I face the animals, who also stand and wait?

E.A. Barton

BAN LIVE EXPORTS!

People chanting, whistles blowing...
"BAN LIVE EXPORTS!"
"BAN LIVE EXPORTS!"
Suddenly there's a terrible silence,
The atmosphere is tense.
I feel nervous and I'm shaking,
I hear a shout!
"THEY'RE COMING!"
In the distance there's a mass of yellow -
The police escort 'just doing their job'.
The lorries crawl along the road,
Coming nearer and nearer.
People yelling and crying -
"MURDERERS!"   "TORTURERS!"
The stench of frightened animals
On their journey to hell.
Their innocent eyes meet mine,
Pleading with me to save them.
I feel so helpless.
It's too late for them,
But we'll never give up.
We'll win one day.
We MUST!

Ross Martin
Age 12

Shoreham's Shame - By a Protester

I have been part of the peaceful protests at Shoreham Harbour since early January. Most of the protesters are like myself; ordinary people who live in the area and who are appalled that such a barbaric trade is being conducted on our doorstep.

Whatever the hour, whatever the weather, there will be a group of people picketing the main port entrance. These range from grandparents to toddlers; those with jobs who attend evenings and weekends; others (like myself) whose commitments are more flexible, appearing at sundry hours of the day or night, depending on the tide times. There is not an hour of the day (or night), when I have not been at Shoreham on one day or other. The atmosphere is good. New friendships flourish as complete strangers converse happily, swapping stories about where they were and what they saw when the last shipment went through; passing information they've learned on: 'they say the ship's on it's way through the lock', and 'do you know about the information line? Just ring 622229 (now changed to 795399) and you get a recorded message telling you what's going on'. They speculate on whether a shipment is imminent: 'Did you see all those police vans parked in that side street down there? They must be going to do it now.' These people are all bound together in a common cause, which unofficially, seems to be shared by many of the police on duty at this port. I have even seen policemen wearing the 'Stop Live Transport' badges.

When the trucks arrive feelings run high. Sometimes they thunder in at a frightening pace. The protesters, penned in on the pavement by a cordon of police, experience a sense of futility; all they can do is shout abuse at the drivers: 'Shame on you' is one of the politer expressions employed on such occasions.

There has been a reduction in the numbers of police deployed for each shipment. due to the prohibitive cost of the operation. Last week, two shipments were delayed slightly when protesters went some way down the Kingsway, past the barriers, and managed to halt the convoy. This meant the trucks came in much more slowly and it was possible to get a clear look at the animals crowded into each truck. The sheep were huddled together, eyes closed, rocking back and forth; obviously terrified. The calves were harder to see but a glimpse of glazed eyes and an occasional intrepid muzzle poking through the slats indicated they were in the same state of distress. Such a sight had a profound effect on the protesters: many cried (including children, whose parents tried to explain that although those animals were going to die, we were there to try to stop more animals dying); some turned their backs as the trucks went through, unable to bear the sight, and, in the case of one lady I spoke to, to avoid having nightmares about it: she said she still saw the terror of the last shipment of animals every time she closed her eyes.

It has now become obvious that the exporters intend to continue this sickening trade, come what may. Even to the point of ignoring police advice and sneaking a convoy in at high speed down the perilous back road, early one Friday morning. (The few police in attendance looked shocked and scared as a near-riot ensued.) The exporters won that battle. Just. But the war's not over yet. As the banners say: 'We're never giving up'.

C. Knox,
February 1995

Sadness

My brothers have been taken,
taken far away.
What's in that horrid lorry?
I hope there's food and hay.
But if there's not,
I wonder what,
is in that horrid lorry,
for them I feel so sorry.
Why are they being taken on such a fine day?
Why are they being taken so far away?

I may only be a sheep,
but in my heart I weep,
for the loss of my brothers.
You cannot see my tears,
in this world full of fears.
In my dreams I see the horrors out at sea,
they're being treated badly,
cramped together so sadly.
Squealing for their mothers,
the babies start to cry.
Some of them just sit there,
Knowing they're going to die.

Lara Bryant
Age 9

Goodbye Humanity

My life is nearly over,
Although it's only just begun
You see, I'm just a poor calf
Snuggled up close to my mum.

There won't be green fields to play in
Or sunshine in open space.
My little friends, I'll see no more
Nor feel the rain upon my face.

For soon, I'll be transported,
And in a crate I'll go
My life will soon be over
To make some villains glow.

If there was compassion and kindness
This world would be a better place
For poor animals who cannot talk,
For all the human race.

A.J.M.
Brighton

Keep a Stiff Upper-Lip

Anxious moments as the back door closes
It's dark and hot as they gasp for air.
Packed like sardines in a wooden box
They're on a roller-coaster death ride
To be murdered en-bloc.
Death traps on moving wheels
The animals sniff at the air
They're crying out for help - but nobody's there.

Now crossing the channel in a watery tomb
Dry-lipped for too many hours.
Some of their friends in a deep sleep
Some still in their mother's womb.
Fear creeps their ample flesh
They're living in hell in perpetual motion
As sentient creatures enmeshed
On a sea of intransigence - unbroken.

They're going to Portugal and Spain
Where matadors wait with their picadors
To greet them with yet still more pain.
On arrival some stumble from the crate
The remainder obviously wait.
Those that are strong enough to walk
Are taken to an inevitable fate.
Some days after leaving our shores
Having been sent on a no-return trip.
The Government stand and do nothing
As they maintain a stiff upper-lip.

Dave Hammond

In a Perfect World...

My name is Anthony Bryant. I am eleven years old and I live in Hove. My family and I have been down to the shipments whenever it has been possible. I have seen hundreds of people, trying desperately to stop the lorries getting past. A large proportion of the protesters are senior citizens and I think they are amazing. They have braved all kinds of weather both day and night, determined to stop this blood trade.

The people who have been arrested, fighting for the rights of animals are very courageous. It is important to stand up for the rights of animals because they have no voice. It makes me very sad and angry to think that man is capable of being so cruel to these poor, innocent animals. The live export issue has alerted many ordinary people of animal cruelty, and hopefully, when we have banned live exports, they will continue to protest against many other animal welfare issues.

In a perfect world, we would not have to protest because animals would roam freely in the wild and everybody would be vegan.

Anthony Bryant
Age 11

Oh! to be in Shoreham
Now that April's there
For whoever waits in Shoreham
Sees with horror and despair
How a tainted ship takes it's living freight
With a nation's shame, to a tiny crate
Which an obscene law should never allow,
In Shoreham, now!

Anonymous

The Port of Shame

My husband and I are ordinary middle class folk who have never done anything spectacular in our lives. - Until January 2nd, 1995.

We are both well into our seventies, but have stood in the cold and wet and windy weather to make our peaceful protest, along with other people, against the live animal transport at the Shoreham port.

We are very proud of what we are doing.

With the help of C.I.W.F., R.S.P.C.A. and I.F.A.W. may this evil trade be swiftly brought to an end.

God Bless all the Animals - and Shame on Shoreham Port.

E. & F.C
Steyning

Creation Abused

English people are reserved, they do not show emotion
Stiff upper lip is still preserved, complying with this notion.
But take a trip to Hove Lagoon and join the people there,
Be it morning, night, or noon, there's people there that care!
The traffic stops, the convoy nears, police are standing guard
The protesters are moved to tears, their access is soon barred.
Livestock crammed, with little space. The journey ends in slaughter
Or in a veal crate, - a disgrace, still used across the water.
The protesters are most distressed at the suffering of these creatures,
Their compassion is so well expressed, as tears adorn their features.
Police escort the lorries through. They say the trade is lawful.
The farmers make 'a bob or two' - we think it's all quite awful.
Scapegoats for the trade are sought, someone to take the blame
But there's only one way to abort these daily trips of shame.
The M.P.'s that we've elected can change the situation
To get the trade rejected by passing legislation.
So, protests today and then again, for justice WILL prevail
The battle will not be in vain, we'll stop these 'trips to Hell'.

Cllr. Leslie A Hamilton
Mayor of Hove

Father God

O dear Father God,
Look down from above,
Send Angels of light
All clothed in your love,
To seek out dark corners,
Where animals wait,
Forsaken, forgotten,
Awaiting their fate.

O may all those men,
Who cause so much pain,
Be filled with such love,
That never again,
Will harm and destruction
Be their shameful deed,
Let love be their master
And kindness their creed.

O Father of love
Hear us as we pray
Your creatures need help
Each hour of the day.
We ask your direction
So please be our guide
To care and sustain them,
Till they reach your side.

Betty Swift

Witness to:

FIRST SHIPMENT OF LIVE ANIMALS FROM
SHOREHAM PORT - 4 JANUARY 1995

The Funeral After Midnight

In the biting wind, in the freezing air,
Human beings full of despair.
The lorries pass through in menacing manner,
Inspite of the many protesters and banners.
Many a scuffle, emotions run high,
Innocent animals are going to die.
One thousand police for controlling the crowd,
Overpowering protesters who shout out loud:
"Ban Live Animal Exports",
"Inhumane, Indecent, Immoral",
"Torture Before Slaughter" and "Shame On You",
Banners held high and our point of view.
To a vantage point looking over the quay,
We watch the ship preparing for sea.
The gentle cargo patiently waits,
While the piercing wind will not abate.
In the sinister darkness and in the distance
The captured cargo can make no resistance.
Our hearts are breaking and our tears flow,
After two hours to load the Northern Cruiser now goes.
Heavy in heart and feeling deepest respect,
Praying out loud there will be no neglect.
We stay with the ship like a funeral procession,
Praying the animals will meet no aggression.
The Northern Cruiser is huge as we stand on the beach,
How powerless we are to protect or reach.
Through the harbour-mouth the captive cargo is taken,
As appeals for compassion are cruelly forsaken.
To veal crates and ritual slaughter their long journeys they must make
However undeserving, the dear animals must partake.
Evidence shows, no mercy is for them,
Brutality not spared again and again.
Agonised and broken, the poor animals are abused,
Whilst blind to benevolence men's intelligence eludes.
The day must come for justice to be done,
With no more suffering and the battle being won.

Liz Taylor

YOU DEMANDED

A little bit of white meat
Where there is no blood or fat
Points to months of torture,
Of animals bred for that.

It never saw the sun rise,
Or saw the dawn of day
But stood on slats - in darkness
Twenty four hours each day.

It stood on slats that slanted,
And slippery at that
It could not even lie down
There was no room for that.

The stench at times was nasty
For there was no fresh air
It yearned for food to give it strength
It yearned for milk as well.

It was taken from its mother
Soon after it was born
And put in total darkness
Until its day of doom.

Six months it stood in darkness
Can you imagine that -
And not even enough room to lie down
To rest its legs and back.

Victoria Lidiard
(submitted by Pauline Wallace)

HOPE

It was Monday the first Monday of 1995
and a new start in my life.
I was at the entrance to Shoreham
Harbour, protesting.
When I met Hope. I had walked off -
Upset, Angry and Sad at what I had seen
The darker side to human nature.
I walked down the port road,
Angry protesters pushing back the live export lorry.
Through the barricades I saw Hope,
I named him.
He stared out through the lorry
His soft brown eyes making contact with mine
For one moment we were one,
We were equal

Him destined for a digestive system
and me for university, a wife, kids?

Looking at Hope suffering
I broke down in tears
So did Hope
I cried, he squealed
I felt helpless so did Hope.
At that moment I knew my life
could never be the same
Hope lived for a reason and now so will I.
I decided during the start of my
bond with Hope to help other
Animals
I couldn't save Hope
And now I know he is suffering.
Hope will not be forgotten.
Every animal I save will be in the name of Hope.
The lorry drivers thought of Hope,
nameless to them,
As one insignificant calf.
But to me and to everything else
I will now do he was much more, he was
courage, he was inspiration
He was HOPE......

David L. Wadman

For David and Hope!

The silence of traffic,
The hush of a crowd.
The deep sickness feeling
When I cry out loud.

These are my feelings,
Day after day,
As I watch the live animals
Get driven away.

Away from their Mothers,
Who cannot protest.
Away from Protesters
Who are doing their best.

Away down the long road
To torture and pain,
Away to starvation,
Being crippled and lame.

Away to a peace,
In the end will succumb.
Away to the light,
Which will welcome them.

They die and they suffer
As a lesson to Man.
Who should lay down his greed,
His pride, when he can.

He should worship, the gift
Of these lives, which he takes,
And realise it's one
Of many mistakes.

For he will suffer
At the end of the day.
When the light will refuse
To pave his way.

Despair I feel, at such
Wicked a thought.
Despair indeed,
Despair at the port.

But I have hope too,
At the courage I see,
Each day as the lorries
Drive, quickly past me

They line up in Convoy,
All nervous with shame.
Cos they need, police escort
As they drive through the rain.

Behind false protection,
They hide and they cower,
Afraid of the truth
And of 'People Power'.

For people in volume
Will win in the end
The people who care
The people who dare.

Let Love and Peace
Surround our cause
Let Light be shone
Over those who applaud.

For Hope and for David
Who have bared their souls
May love be the answer
To all of your goals.

Di White.

We, The Protesters (alias "Mob Rule")

From Brussels comes the latest demand to the Government. " You must control your protesters". How long will it be before we are allowed to do nothing but stand on the pavement with our heads bowed and our spirits suffocated by injustice?

The Red Ship called 'The Northern Cruiser', once a seal-culling ship will live in the minds of those of us who have watched the last truck forcing its way into her hold, letting down its tyres to accommodate its pathetic cargo, and each time she sails she takes with her a fragment of our democracy, the banners are already asking, "Where is Britain?"

Pussy cat, pussy cat, where have you been? I've been to London to see the Queen. The Queen? What Queen?

Carla Lane

Where Are They Now?

Where are they now those thousands of animals
Who pass by us imprisoned in lorries.
With soft faces small, with soft faces large,
With pleading eyes they ask us for help.
Communicating desperation from animal to human,
Communicating desperation from human to animal.
What can we do, our powers are little.
To release them our wish, but our hands are tied.
Not even to touch are we allowed.
Not even a comfort can we extend.
We talk to them as we run with the lorries.
We say we care, we say we are sorry.
Whatever the circumstance they keep their dignity,
Whatever is forced upon them by man's inhumanity.
No longer in fields they pass by us in lorries,
Betrayed by Britain and banished abroad.
Traumatic their journeys and at the mercy of ruthlessness,
Brutality abounds this so called animal husbandry.
Although it is Spring now, most fields are empty
And many are brown instead of green.
Britain's blue skies are emerging from grey
And the sun is warming for it is nearly May.
The animals' backs should be feeling sun's warmth
And the animals' tummies digesting green grass.
Instead of that, the fields are empty
And the beautiful animals have been rejected.
Where are they now, I dread to think.
I think of them often and I hope they are safe,
But I am afraid they are not, is most animals' fate,
For intensive farming has created this state
And European subsidies have made it much worse.
To see the fields empty is a depressing sight.
A loss for the animals and a loss for us.
Animals enrich our quality of life
And in any case, we should do what is right.
No cruelty and a comfortable life.
Where are they now? Let them be alright.

Liz Taylor

Can't You See It's Evil?

How long must this evil trade go on for?
How many nights must we stand here in the rain,
Can we put our hope in politicians,
Will our hopes be washed out down the drain.

I've watched the lorries take the calves through,
Floods of tears won't stop their misery and pain,
It breaks my heart to see them suffer,
What does it take to change the minds of men.

Can't you see it's evil
My mind's pictures are driving me insane.
Can't you see it's evil,
Too many people want to see this end.

You gave your life to save the animals,
Not many men would go the distance that you do.
Look to the hills to cleanse your soul,
Look to your side and she'll be waiting there for you.

Can't you see it's evil
My mind's pictures are driving me insane.
Can't you see it's evil,
Too many people want to see this end.

"I've learned our lives are filled with changes,
We turn our thoughts to where life is so unfair,
So let's join forces in this venture,
Let the world know how much we care."

Words & Music by
T.J.Drewett
March 1995

Consider

Consider the case of the Factory Farm
We are told that the animals come to no harm.

Yet the hens are unable to stretch out their wings,
They squat in cramped cages like prisoners, poor things.

The veal calves die young, for the sweet meat they yield
Without ever smelling a summertime field.

And litters of pigs live in foul stinking stalls,
With nothing to look at but concrete block walls.

Consider the case of people who eat
Their factory farmed bacon, cheap eggs and white meat.

The creatures who suffer, do so for Man's greed -
Consider the animals. Consider THEIR need.

Tracy

'To Hell'

They took me from my mother,
I was only three days old,
Sent off to the market
For sixty-five pounds sold.

Bundled on a lorry
With many of my kind,
Feeling sad and frightened,
My mother left behind.

We travelled many hours
Before we saw the sea,
Met by several people,
Reaching sadly out to me.

Some shouted at the drivers
Showing anger and despise,
Compassion in their souls,
Tears welling in their eyes.

They tried to block the road,
Were outnumbered by the police
Tools used by the government
Applied to keep the peace?

The lorries grinded to a halt
Just beside the berth,
Blind eyes peered in on us
I ask you, "What's that worth?" £££

The bow door pulled up
In total darkness now,
We set sail on the high seas,
The destination - HELL!

J.E.M.

People Who Care

Every day the people who care,
Come on to the streets just to share.
They make demonstrations that fill the Sussex air,
And the animals hear them and know they are there.

The hundreds of people that come to protest,
Really and truly are doing their best;
They hope they will win and freedom will reign,
And animals will live without fear again.

We'll never give up while live exports go on,
We know in our hearts that it's all very wrong.
We may shout and may scream, but we only mean well,
So we'll never give in for we know time will tell.

Dominic Ferris
Age 9

The Funeral Cortege

In the distance I see the lorries
carrying the corpses of the future
For you, no dignified silence, flowers,
no love and respect
Just us to mourn your passing.
As you go by I see your face,
smell the fear and sense the terror.
My heart and soul are torn apart
and inside, I cry a thousand tears.
Tomorrow, because of their greed
there will be another funeral cortege.

Mark

A Prayer

"Animal Heaven"

PLEASE -
Save the animals from suffering,
Free them from the cruelty of Man,
Take them to a world beyond
Untouched by human hand.
A world of light, love and peace,
To the sanctuary of eternal love,
No man can ever reach, -

"Animal Heaven".

Amen.

Jacqueline

The Calf

I glanced at mum, I saw her pain,
As the lorries came -
The anguish in her eyes -
Then she let out a sad sigh.

She cried out "please let me keep one!
All the others have gone."
There is no kindness in their hearts,
"No, now is the time you must part."

Then with sadness she looked away,
So now I must pray,
Pray for the day when Man must see
That he is living dangerously.

Then the long journey began,
To a far-away land,
I look ahead, what do I see?
A long, cruel end for me.

Suddenly the spirits from above
Call out in anger, "there is no love!"
There is a lesson in all this -
May there be forgiveness........

S.E. Deble

A "Wake"

All creatures great and small
Are sent to fulfil us all,
To give us joy, and not for taste,
To pull their horns off, just for waste.

To hear their screams and cries for help
As Man puts on his act from hell
These little things, just like us
Are sent from God to be here, in this place.

Like You and Me, and Him and Us,
These creatures are a must,
So don't think twice, think three or four
Do we need them, or them for us.

Their cries and sorrows we must mourn
For tomorrow they will know no dawn,
Dawn has broken, no more sounds
The fields are empty all around.

We stand and gaze and wonder why
Wonder, and wonder and wonder, Oh! Why?

Gillian Phillips

Operation Ferndown
© Stewart Weir 1995

Waiting For The Ride Home
© M.E. Austin 1995

Three To One
© M.E. Austin

Doing It The Hard Way
© M.E. Austin 1995

A Law Unto Themselves

The incident referred to occurred at about 5 a.m. on Saturday, 28th January. It appeared that ITF were advised by Senior Police not to proceed with that morning's shipment, but did so, regardless.

On this bitterly cold morning, as protesters were still joining those who had stood at the port entrance for most of the night, the Convoy entered via the slip road at Butts Wharf. For perhaps no more than a second or two, most of us stared in disbelief. The usual sign indicating an imminent shipment; the steady build up of police, had not occured. However, we weren't static for long - Within moments, forty odd protesters clad in thick layers of clothing jumped over the fences and charged in full cry towards the roundabout behind the Adur public house. A combination of adrenaline, the wind and sheer determination saw to it that only one lorry turned the corner without facing opposition.

With no regard for their unfortunate cargo, let alone the lives of the brave people who had made their way on to the road, the drivers accelerated, deliberately swinging their vehicles from one side to the other in an attempt to flatten anyone in their way. As the trucks passed, cars full of masked guards waving bats and coshes pulled out of the darkness to provide security, while the surprised, few police sat in their vans asleep or drinking tea. Chasing after the convoy, anger and frustration overcame us - anger because we had witnessed the increasingly ugly nature of all those involved in this trade - frustration because with a few more people or the right positioning we may have been able to halt the trucks.

After the heat of anger subsided, even after sleep I found myself in a state of shock. Not just because of the helplessness and utter frustration at being unable to stop the abusers but as a reaction to the way I feel this time. Several days before, when the convoy passed, I cried for the first time - because of sadness, anger or sheer exhaustion, I don't know. Perhaps I had been too close to the trapped animals. This time, I didn't cry; nobody did. We couldn't see the faces of the frightened creatures, only glimpses as the lorries hurtled by. My reaction was of violent anger. I wanted to hurt these people and their masked escorts and when they had passed, I released my frustration on the fences there to control us.

Shouting across the water as the animals were being loaded aboard the ship, I realised compassion had become mixed with hatred. How can any decent person remain unconcerned by this? I've changed. It makes me feel uncomfortable but nevertheless this anger remains absolutely right and justifiable.

Martin Reddin

Twentieth Century Policing

Why do you say it?

We know why

Why do you do it?

We know why

You like to see the people cry
You like to see them wracked with pain
People distressed again and again
The State has scrambled your brain.

Emotions torn and anger strong
You seem not to care or know what's wrong.
Of feelings for others, you are devoid
You've been programmed, 'Humanoid'.
You obey without question,
Your duty you do
We feel great sadness and pity for you.
No conscience, no morals have you left
Of care for God's creatures you are bereft.

Eddie Roberts

Basin Road South

Police chopper flying overhead
Becomes a sound we've come to dread.
Soon the trucks come down the road,
Wall to wall with pathetic load.
Baby calves, hungry, tired and wet
Sea trip to Dieppe to conquer yet.
Sheep, packed tight in trucks behind,
No loving shepherd to treat them kind.
Just policemen in riot gear, jet black,
Running side by side, front to back.
Protesters shouting out in vain,
Poor creatures going for ill gotten gain.
How long before Waldegrave takes heed
And sees these creatures, from their torture freed?

Cllr. Bob Carden

What a Waste of Money!

It all began when we saw the pictures on the news.
A feeling struck our hearts.
Seeing the animals suffering in unbelievable ways.
We couldn't bear it, so we went down to the port.
Our first shipment was confusing.
Everybody is chatting and laughing.
But, when the policemen block the roads
It goes silent.
The atmosphere is eerie and thick.
I hear the hiss of a lorry's brakes.
The animals are coming through.
Then, "SCUM", "SHAME ON YOU", and " BEEP"!
I don't know what to do.
My brain is whizzing around my head.
Suddenly, it's all over and it was like a dream.
Everybody is shouting "SHAME!"
People crying.
Everytime the policevans come into sight, people shout,
"WHAT A WASTE OF MONEY!!!!!"

BAN LIVE EXPORTS

Lewis Porter
Age 8

I have read somewhere a couple of lines that I think could be appropriate for the animals that are exported:

We are the unwilling -
Led by the unqualified -
Doing the unnecessary -
For the ungrateful.

Author Unknown
Submitted by Iris Gyure

Little Calf

Where are you now, little calf, where are you now?
I saw you looking at me as the lorries swept past.
The look in your eyes I cannot wipe from my mind
And the terrible suffering that awaits you and your kind.
You are doomed from birth and so is your mother
As she is made to have one after another.
The greed of man will go on for ever
But we will not give up our fight or endeavour.
As you await your fate on some distant shore
The profits and politics of man we abhor.
Please some one listen, before they send
Many more little calves to this, their horrific end.

A. Williams

Evil Gain

When creatures are born to this world of human sin
They have no idea of the trouble they are in.
With the farmers, exporters and landowners galore
Whose pact with the devil, good people abhor.
Men who'll cause them much suffering, torture and pain
And distress to protesters again and again.

Why must newly born lambs, calves, pigs and sheep
Travel for days without food, drink or sleep
Must they suffer the stress, misery and pain
Just to line pockets for greedy mens gain.

I'm referring to M.P.'s and Lords etc, in bed
With those savages I've mentioned before,
They believe it's O.K. cos the law's on their side
But that's just a smokescreen behind which they hide.

They are wielding their power, their influence, their cash
To order policemen, protesters to bash
Into submission, the protest to stop.
But we will continue to care and protest
At these convoys of evil, and put to the test
The incarnate devil enshrined in these thugs,
Who devoid of the morals of civilised men
Send calves into veal crates - a torturous pen.

They care only for money and money again
I truly believe they must be insane.
The law that supports them could not care less
They kick and they punch and throw us aside
Behind "Its our duty", they all try to hide.

Yellow vests arrest us, put us to the test
But we know that we're right and will come off best.
Now hear this, our message, you grey, sad, sick men
We will win this war cos we're morally right
And our strength will increase, now the end is in sight.

Eddie Roberts

The Tree

I massive stand in docile strength
And let you come to me.
My trunk shall be your highway
Branches your cradle
Leaves your larder
And in my shade shall you leap and skip.

My bare arms stretch in agony.
Rigid, my shadow falls
Across the centuries.
Long nails are driven in the wood.
Be still, you cannot move.
Your young limbs shall never move again.

Pearl Garton
Somerset

Veal Calf

Look into my eyes
Tell me what you see
Mine is a 'life' of suffering
A pain without end,
Chained, tethered, caged
In darkness do I stand
My sentence for the 'crime' of being
excess to demand.
To them I am worth **nothing**
Until I am dead,
My veal crate is a living death,
Please hear my silent cries
Of misery,
Don't let me die in vain,
Please Please fight on to save
All calves from pain.

Jacqueline

Facts Not Fiction

To the people who go down to the port entrance every day that a shipment is expected, the protest as Shoreham is more than just 'another protest'. They are there to make a statement. - a statement that it should not be necessary to have to make; "Ban Live Exports".

Daily, we fight our way through an intricate web of evidence gatherers, police in riot gear and yellow coats, (sometimes outnumbering us four to one), and police vehicles, to make our feelings clear to the men who drive the livestock trucks. Others do whatever they can in an attempt to stop the trucks passing through. Every day, we witness scenes which before, many have only seen on television or in films. We do things that we never thought possible or that we doubted we were capable of. As tempers flare, we are picked off one by one, never to return. A swiftly served exclusion order sees to that. But still, our spirit is not broken. You can't divide a group of people who have come together for the same purpose.

Every avenue of life is represented - invisible bridges, unconsciously built over a period months, span the gulfs created by the dictates of society until now, there are no differences. We cannot be divided nor separated. We are a single body, unanimous in our goal...propping each other up when things get tough. Young men look after the elderly, like surrogate sons. Old men relive the days when their limbs were as strong as their minds and women who met here as strangers, comfort each other as the convoy passes. This protest is built on compassion, not only for the animals destined for Europe and further, but for each other.

We are the sound of the voice of the people who cry "no more.." We will not be silenced in the face of temporary defeat, and in our anguish we grow more determined... 'Unlawful' our protest might be, but moral it most certainly is.

Laughing lorry drivers, balaclava-ed cowards masquerading as security guards, jibes from a certain element within the police force - we've suffered them all.

Our foundations are battered away from all sides. Classed as hoodlums, thugs, 'rent-a-mob' and extremists, but still we stand firm. Every so-called 'mistake' that we make is blown out of all proportion. No matter what is said about us, no matter who tries to discredit the actions of anyone down there, regardless of the media hype and the power of those behind this wretched trade and the people who condone it, we will remain strong in our belief that the cause for which we fight is right and just. The few who oppose what we stand for will come to see that.

Wenda
